TOP 10 FOOTBALL RUSHERS

William W. Lace

SPORTS TOP 10

Enslow Publishers, Inc.

40 Industrial Road   PO Box 38
Box 398   Aldershot
Berkeley Heights, NJ 07922 Hants GU12 6BP
USA   UK

http://www.enslow.com

Library of Congress Cataloging-in-Publication Data

Lace, William W.
    Top 10 football rushers / William W. Lace.
       p. cm. — (Sports top 10)
    ISBN 0-89490-519-8
    1. Running backs (Football)—United States—Biography—Juvenile literature.
    2. National Football League—History—Juvenile literature. [1. Football players.
    2. National Football League.] I. Title. II. Title: Top 10 football rushers. III. Series.
    GV939.A1L336 1994
    796.332'092'2—dc20
    [B]   93-40470
                                      CIP
                                       AC

Printed in the United States of America

1 0 9 8 7 6 5

Photo Credits: AP/Wide World Photos, pp. 30, 35, 41; Photo by Tom Albert, p. 33;
Chicago Bears, p. 27; © Chicago Tribune, p. 29, 37; Cleveland Browns, p. 9; Dallas
Cowboys Weekly, pp. 19, 21, 43, 45; Photo Courtesy of Houston Oilers, pp. 11, 13;
Official Raiders Photo, pp. 14, 17; Pittsburgh Steelers/Michael F. Fabus, pp. 22, 25; The
Plain Dealer, Cleveland, Ohio, p. 6; Photo by Bob Smith, p. 38.

Cover Photo: Photo by Tom Albert.

Interior Design: Richard Stalzer.

CONTENTS

INTRODUCTION

ONE AFTERNOON IN THE YEAR 1823 the boys of Rugby School in England were playing a game of "football." (This is something like the game we know in the United States as soccer.) The object was to kick the ball over your opponents' goal line.

The game was scoreless. It was getting dark. Then, instead of kicking the ball, a boy named William Webb Ellis tucked it under his arm and ran! Before the other team knew what had happened, he crossed its goal.

Soon, running became the most important part of a new game, rugby. And rugby is what turned into American football.

The running back is the basic building block of any football team. In a football game, the offensive team tries to establish the run. The defense's first job is to stop the run. "Football is, and always will be, a running game first," said Vince Lombardi, the former Green Bay Packers and Washington Redskins coach.[1]

Running is what makes football a rugged, physical sport. Without the running, football would be a tame contest of pitch and catch. "Football without running," author Murray Olderman wrote, "is only a kind of glorified frisbee."[2]

The position of running back does not usually have the glamour or the salary of quarterback. But, the running back is frequently the best athlete on the team. Even in grade school or junior high school, the player who has the right combination of size, speed, and quickness is the one who will carry the ball.

The running back is a target from the moment he takes the ball. A quarterback can retreat, but he cannot. He has to take the punishment of two, three, or four people hitting him at once. He is expected to break tackles, to bounce off. Above all, he is expected to be slammed into but not lose the ball.

Some people might say choosing the top ten running backs is easy. Just pick the men with the top ten career rushing totals. It's not that simple. If you did that, Gale Sayers would be missing. His career was cut short by an injury. Many think he was the best of them all, though.

And, if you simply take the career leaders, you ignore today's players. Players like Barry Sanders and Emmitt Smith. They have clearly shown that they're among the best.

Running backs are like snowflakes. No two are just exactly alike. One may be a 150-pound scatback. Another may be a 250-pound bulldozer. They may glide like Eric Dickerson, prance like Walter Payton, cut on a dime like Sayers, or run smack over you like Jim Brown. Each has his own special style.

It takes a special kind of person to be a ball carrier. "All running backs are bonded together by ties not known to those who've never carried the ball," said Jim Brown. "We all have our Ph.D.s in running."[3]

CAREER STATISTICS

Player	Seasons	Attempts	Yards	Average	Touchdowns (Rushing)
JIM BROWN	9	2,359	12,312	5.22	106
EARL CAMPBELL	8	2,187	9,407	4.30	74
ERIC DICKERSON	11	2,996	13,259	4.43	90
TONY DORSETT	12	2,936	12,739	4.34	77
FRANCO HARRIS	13	2,949	12,120	4.11	91
WALTER PAYTON	13	3,838	16,726	4.36	110
BARRY SANDERS	9	2,719	13,778	5.07	95
GALE SAYERS	7	991	4,956	5.00	39
O.J. SIMPSON	11	2,404	11,236	4.67	61
EMMITT SMITH	8	2,595	11,234	4.33	112

JIM BROWN

Brown goes over the top against the St. Louis Cardinals. Brown was bigger than most running backs and could bully his way to a first down.

JIM BROWN

JIM BROWN WROTE THAT HE was "born to be a fullback."[1] He was almost an end instead. He didn't do much in his freshman year at Syracuse University. Coach Ben Schwartzwalder asked him to go out for end in his sophomore year.

Brown said he didn't want to play end. He was a running back. The coach gave in. If Brown had not been so stubborn, he might never have been one of the greatest runners in the history of the NFL.

Brown didn't even go to college on a scholarship. Kenneth Molloy was from Brown's home town of Manhasset, New York. He was also a graduate of Syracuse University. He convinced Brown to turn down more than forty offers from other schools and attend Syracuse in upstate New York. Molloy got several businessmen in Manhasset to pay his way his freshman year, but Brown didn't know this.

Brown had come a long way in more ways than one. He grew up on little St. Simons Island off the coast of Georgia. His mother went to New York when Jim was two. His father drifted in and out of young Jimmy's life. Brown lived on St. Simons until he was nine. Then he joined his mother in New York.

They lived in Manhasset on Long Island. It was there that Brown discovered sports. He was head of a teenage gang in high school. He said later, "there were many times when I came perilously close to becoming a no-account."[2] Instead, he put his energy into football, basketball, lacrosse, and track. He wound up at Syracuse.

Coach Schwartzwalder did not regret keeping Brown at

running back. He was second in the nation in rushing when he was a junior, and he was All-American as a senior. He led Syracuse to the Cotton Bowl; there he scored four touchdowns but Syracuse lost. *Sport* magazine named him College Football Player of the Year for 1956.

He was drafted in 1957 by the Cleveland Browns. As a rookie, he led the league in rushing with 942 yards. That was more than 200 yards ahead of the second place running back. He also helped the Browns to the Eastern Division championship. He was the first rookie ever to lead the voting for the NFL all-star team.

He led the league in rushing again in 1958. In fact, he was the top rusher in the NFL in eight of the nine years he played. In 1962, the only year he didn't win the rushing title, he finished third. His 126 touchdowns (rushing and receiving) are still an NFL record.

Brown was one of the few players who retired at the peak of his career. He led the NFL with 1,544 rushing yards in 1965, then left football to star in movies.

Jim Brown had the perfect combination of size and speed. He was a fullback for most of his pro career, and he could bull his way for short yardage. One opponent commented on Brown's strength. After a game he said, "I had one of my best days against Jim Brown. I made almost as much yardage as he did—riding on his back."[3]

But, if a hole opened up, he had the speed to break the long gainer, and he had the moves to get open. Another opponent said, "He's the only player I know who can run faster sideways than straight ahead."[4]

Brown had endurance, too. He averaged over 250 carries per season. "He was much bigger, much stronger than me," wrote Gale Sayers. "He was the kind of man who could carry the ball 40 times a game, and I wasn't that kind of man."[5]

JIM BROWN

BORN: February 17, 1936, St. Simons Island, Georgia.

HIGH SCHOOL: Manhasset High School, Manhasset, New York.

COLLEGE: Syracuse University.

PRO: Cleveland Browns, 1957–1965.

RECORDS: NFL Record for Career Touchdowns, 126 (106, Rushing; 20, Receiving).

HONORS: NFL Rookie of the Year, 1957.
Pro Football Hall of Fame, 1971.

In his nine seasons in Cleveland, Brown led the league in rushing eight times and he still holds the record for the most touchdowns scored. Coach Paul Brown called him, "The greatest runner in football history."

EARL CAMPBELL

SOMEHOW, EARL CAMPBELL ALWAYS FOUND the right path—when he was a troubled youngster, an out-of-shape college star, an exhausted pro running back. It was as if the prayer his mother taught him—"Lord, lift me up"—was answered.[1]

For instance, there was the game against the Miami Dolphins. Campbell was a rookie with the Houston Oilers. He had already carried the ball 27 times for 118 yards and he was very tired. But Houston only led by five points. Campbell was called on once again.

He took a pitchout from quarterback Dan Pastorini, hit the hole, and suddenly found himself in the open. Somehow, he discovered the strength to put on a burst of speed. He dashed 81 yards for the game-clinching touchdown. He had reached deep within himself to overcome difficulty.

Campbell had difficulty of another kind when he was growing up in Tyler, Texas. He started skipping school when he was fourteen. He began smoking cigarettes, drinking, and making money shooting pool. But the lessons his mother, Ann, had taught Earl and his ten brothers and sisters came to his rescue. He knew he was headed down a dangerous road. He thought about his mother's prayer, and he decided that sports was the way he could be lifted up.

He became an all-state running back, and then set rushing records his freshman and sophomore years at the University of Texas. When he was a junior he suffered a leg injury, and he couldn't play most of that year. He got out of shape. He ended up 40 pounds above his playing weight of 220.

One day, a small boy who attended Campbell's church

EARL CAMPBELL

Campbell looks for an opening to rush downfield. His super leg power let him run over instead of around tacklers, many times dragging them along for extra yards.

gave him a sign. It read, "Keep me going, Lord." Campbell vowed to get into shape. In his senior year, he gained more than 1,700 yards. He also won the Heisman Trophy as the country's best college football player.

Campbell was the first player taken in the 1978 NFL draft. He was chosen by the Houston Oilers. It didn't take them long to find out they had made the right pick. In his first pro game, Campbell ran 73 yards for a touchdown on his third carry. He wound up with 137 yards and he went on to become the first rookie since Jim Brown to lead the league in rushing.

Campbell was never a shifty back, like Gale Sayers or Walter Payton. His success was based on a combination of size and speed. "He is as fast as one of those 170-pound scatbacks," said former Arkansas coach Frank Broyles. "When you put 220 pounds on something that fast, you have something no one has ever seen."[2]

His tremendous leg drive was propelled by his enormous thighs. He slammed into tacklers, often dragging them with him for extra yards. "You get your shoulder into his hip," said Dallas Cowboys lineman Larry Cole, "and it seems like that hip is giving you a forearm."[3]

Campbell's power was complemented by speed and balance. Houston quarterback Dan Pastorini described him: "Earl runs like he's got a rocket tied to his tail and a gyroscope in his stomach."[4]

He was a complete player for Houston, but the wear and tear finally got to him. He led the American Football Conference his first four years in professional football. But injuries gradually slowed him to a stop. He retired after the 1986 season. He had played only eight years in the NFL.

Someone once asked Houston coach Bum Phillips if Campbell was in a class by himself. Phillips replied that, whatever class Earl was in, "It don't take long to call roll."[5]

EARL CAMPBELL

BORN: March 29, 1955, Tyler, Texas.

HIGH SCHOOL: John Tyler High School, Tyler, Texas.

COLLEGE: University of Texas.

PRO: Houston Oilers, 1978–1986.

HONORS: Heisman Trophy Winner, 1977.
NFL Rookie of the Year (AFC), 1978.
Pro Football Hall of Fame, 1991.

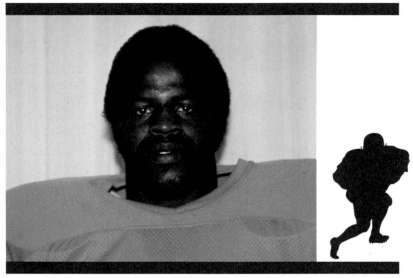

Winning the Heisman Trophy and being the first player picked in the 1978 NFL draft were only the beginning of Campbell's record-breaking career. One of the league's top rushers, Campbell retired because of injuries in 1986.

ERIC DICKERSON

Dickerson squeaks through a hole in the Dallas defense. Rather than faking out his tacklers like other running backs, Dickerson ran with blazing speed to make first downs.

Eric Dickerson

ONE NIGHT, ERIC DICKERSON DREAMED he gained 2,001 yards in one season. It was a nightmare. At the time, he was closing in on O. J. Simpson's record of 2,003 yards. His dream was two yards short!

After the next Sunday, he didn't have to worry any more. Late in the game, quarterback Jeff Kemp called a play named "47 gap." When Dickerson's Los Angeles Rams broke the huddle, tackle Bill Bain said, "This is for you, Eric. This is yours."[1]

Dickerson took the handoff. He saw a hole, turned on the speed, and swept around the right end for nine yards. He had done it! He had now gained 2,007 yards. The next week Dickerson added 98 more yards to wind up the season with 2,105.

Dickerson had always been the best. In his first junior high game in Sealy, Texas, he scored four touchdowns. "Suddenly, people were looking at me differently," he remembered. "Their eyes showed respect."[2] He gained 2,642 yards in high school. He was called one of two or three of the greatest players in the country.

Dickerson attended Southern Methodist University in Dallas. He shared running duties with another player, but he still broke Earl Campbell's Southwest Conference career rushing record.

The Rams made Dickerson the second pick in the 1983 draft. In training camp, coach John Robinson thought he looked slow. He didn't know then that Dickerson ran so smoothly that he didn't appear to be running fast. "He's an extremely powerful runner, but he's so graceful that it's really deceiving," Robinson said. "He's the smoothest runner I've ever seen."[3]

Dickerson led the NFL in rushing three of his first four seasons. In 1987, however, he had a bitter contract argument with the Rams. He was then traded to Indianapolis. With Dickerson in their backfield, the Colts made the playoffs for the first time in ten years.

Dickerson's style was unusual. He ran almost straight up rather than moving low to the ground. He didn't rely on moves or fakes; he relied on his blazing speed. "Eric makes it easy for us," Rams guard David Hill said once. "He hits the line quick, and that's the best thing that can happen for an offensive lineman. With another back, you feel you have to hold a block longer."[4]

Because of his speed, he was a threat to score on every play. "Every time Dickerson gets the ball," former New England Patriots coach Raymond Berry said, "you don't breathe until he's tackled."[5]

Dickerson's speed was somewhat surprising because of the extra weight he carried. To protect himself from tacklers, he wore a large face mask, a neck collar, a flak jacket, and extra-heavy shoulder pads. The extra gear weighed more than twenty pounds.

Eric had problems off the field. He was unhappy with his contract in Indianapolis, so he went to the Los Angeles Raiders before the 1992 season. Then, before the 1993 season, he was traded to the Atlanta Falcons.

O. J. Simpson once said, "Dickerson is the best I've ever seen. He should end up with all the records."[6] It was not to be. Dickerson was traded to the Green Bay Packers in October 1993. He failed his physical examination at Green Bay and decided to retire from football. In 11 seasons, he had rushed for 13,259 yards, second only to Walter Payton's 16,726.

Eric Dickerson

BORN: September 2, 1960, Sealy, Texas.

HIGH SCHOOL: Sealy High School, Sealy, Texas.

COLLEGE: Southern Methodist University.

PRO: Los Angeles Rams, 1983–1987; Indianapolis Colts,
    1987–1991; Los Angeles Raiders, 1991–1993;
    Atlanta Falcons, 1993.

HONORS: NFL Rookie of the Year (NFC), 1983.

Although Dickerson never played on a championship team, he was consistently rated one of the top rushers in the NFL. He holds the record for the most yards rushed in a season, and ended his eleven-year career second only to Walter Payton in total yards.

TONY DORSETT

THE DALLAS COWBOYS WERE BACKED up to their own one-yard line. They ran the "31-fold" play. This called for Tony Dorsett to slant off right tackle. The Minnesota Vikings defense was drawn in tight. Dorsett took the handoff, but he saw that his path was blocked. He cut to his left and squirted through the line into the open field.

Teammate Drew Pearson blocked one defender about midfield, but another defender tried to push Dorsett out of bounds. Dorsett stayed in. He kept his balance and completed the ninety-nine-yard run. This set an NFL record that can never be broken. "It will always be one of my greatest moments in football," he wrote later.[1]

There weren't too many great moments when Dorsett first played football when he was a child in Aliquippa, Pennsylvania. He was scared of getting hurt. He would drag his pants in the dirt after Midget League games. He wanted his older brothers to think he had played more than he really had.

He got some experience and grew larger. Then he became a star running back. In his senior year at Hopewell High School, Dorsett gained 1,244 yards and scored 23 touchdowns. The initials of his name and his ability to score led to his nickname—TD.

He went to college at the University of Pittsburgh. It was just a few miles from Aliquippa. He set the all-time major college career rushing record of 6,082 yards. He was the first college player ever to rush for more than 1,000 yards in each of his four years. In his senior-year season, he led his team to the national championship, and he won the Heisman

TONY DORSETT

Dorsett slips through the hands of a Tampa Bay defender. Dorsett became one the first running backs to escape his tacklers using a 360-degree spin.

trophy. He ended his college career by leading Pitt to a 27–3 Sugar Bowl victory over Georgia Tech.

In 1977, the Dallas Cowboys traded four draft choices so they could move up in the draft. They wanted to get Dorsett. The Cowboys thought a flashy runner like Dorsett would help them win the Super Bowl.

Dorsett made an immediate impression. "I saw his ability from the first day," said Dan Reeves. Reeves was a Cowboys assistant coach at the time. "He was getting open without using fakes. He was just a blur against the linebackers."[2]

Rookie Dorsett gained more than 1,000 yards. And the Cowboys beat the Denver Broncos in Super Bowl XII. Dorsett spent eleven seasons in Dallas. He gained more than 1,000 yards eight times. He was traded to Denver in 1988. In his final year, he moved into second place on the all-time rushing list.

He had great speed, but he had even greater acceleration. He would loaf along behind his blockers. If even a tiny hole appeared, he zoomed through it and was gone.

He was one of the most slippery runners in history, with more than his share of fancy moves. He was one of the first to do a 360-degree spin on a regular basis. "It's exhilarating to get out of the way and make them [tacklers] miss," he said.[3]

He also could change direction without losing a lot of speed. "He doesn't run," said former sportscaster Howard Cosell, "He glides."[4]

Chicago Bears general manager, Jim Finks, added, "The reason Dorsett strikes fear into everybody is that he has that rare ability to start and stop, plus the ability to go all the way at any time."[5] In 1994, Tony Dorsett was elected to the Pro Football Hall of Fame.

Tony Dorsett

BORN: April 7, 1954, Aliquippa, Pennsylvania.

HIGH SCHOOL: Hopewell High School, Aliquippa, Pennsylvania.

COLLEGE: University of Pittsburgh.

PRO: Dallas Cowboys, 1977–1987; Denver Broncos, 1988.

RECORDS: NFL Record (tie) for Longest Run from Scrimmage, 99 yards.

HONORS: Heisman Trophy Winner, 1976; NFL Rookie of the Year (NFC), 1977; Pro Football Hall of Fame, 1994.

Dorsett helped the Dallas Cowboys win Super Bowl XII his rookie year. His combination of fancy moves and exceptional speed made him one of the most dangerous running backs in the NFL.

FRANCO HARRIS

Winning four Super Bowls with the Pittsburgh Steelers, Harris consistently ran for more than 1,000 yards each season. He also earned two of professional football's highest awards, Rookie of the Year and Super Bowl MVP.

FRANCO HARRIS

FRANCO HARRIS' RUNNING STYLE WAS to wait. He would glide along the line of scrimmage until a hole opened. Then he exploded through it. All good things, they say, come to him who waits. Harris waited, and good things came.

Harris was not considered the best back on his college team. Lydell Mitchell was. But, Harris waited. He was taken first in the NFL draft. He had a much better professional career than Mitchell.

On Harris' most famous play, his Pittsburgh Steelers were all but dead. They trailed the Oakland Raiders, 7–6. There were only twenty-two seconds left, and the ball was on their own forty-yard line. Quarterback Terry Bradshaw threw a pass to John Fuquay, but a Raider swatted it away.

But, there was Harris—waiting. He scooped up the ball just before it hit the ground and flew the last 42 yards for the winning touchdown. Later he said, "I just happened to be in the right place at the right time."[1]

Harris grew up in New Jersey. He was 6 feet 3 inches tall and weighed 215 pounds when he was a high school sophomore. He was so fast, though, that nobody thought about making him a lineman.

He played in Mitchell's shadow at Penn State University. But the scouts knew who was the better pro prospect. Harris was chosen first. "We were looking for someone with size, speed, and catching ability," said Steelers coach Chuck Noll. "Franco was our man."[2]

Harris didn't disappoint his coach. He gained more than 1,000 yards his first year. He was named Rookie of the Year in 1972. He was injured in 1973, but the next year he helped

Pittsburgh win its first-ever NFL championship. He gained 158 yards on 34 carries in the Super Bowl IX victory over Minnesota. He was named Most Valuable Player for that game.

Harris played nine more seasons, and he won three more Super Bowls with the Steelers. He had eight seasons in which he chalked up more than 1,000 yards; this was a record. He never led the league or his conference in rushing. Yet, his career total of 12,120 yards is the fifth best ever.

Harris was one of the most popular players in Steeler history. He spoke to groups of young people, telling them to stay in school. He gave money and volunteer time to the local Boys Clubs. Pittsburgh fans formed a club. They called it "Franco's Italian Army."

His running style was unusual for a man his size. He didn't try to run through or over people. He waited—looking for a hole. He was a power runner when he had to be. But he did say, "If it's a matter of winding up in the same place, I'd rather not get hit than get hit, chicken as that may sound."[3]

Even though he did not particularly enjoy getting hit, "if there is no hole, you get what you can get."[4] He had so much power that he often got much more than anyone expected.

"It's unbelievable how he gets away from tacklers," said Minnesota coach Bud Grant. "Just when you think you have him stopped, he rips away for 20 yards."[5]

Harris said, midway through his rookie year, "I had the confidence, and I had the ability, but I wondered how long it would take before it all came out."[6]

All he had to do, it turned out, was wait.

FRANCO HARRIS

BORN: March 7, 1950, Fort Dix, New Jersey.

HIGH SCHOOL: Rancocas Valley Regional High School, Mount Holly,
New Jersey.

COLLEGE: Pennsylvania State University.

PRO: Pittsburgh Steelers, 1972–1984.

HONORS: NFL Rookie of the Year (AFC), 1972.
Most Valuable Player, Super Bowl IX.
Pro Football Hall of Fame, 1990.

Harris darts past his defender. Although Harris had the size and strength to take hits from tacklers, he often waited at the line of scrimmage for an opening before he started running.

WALTER PAYTON

THE PLAY WAS "TOSS 28 weak." The Chicago Bears' Walter Payton had run it hundreds of times. This 1984 run against the New Orleans Saints, however, would go down in history.

Bears' quarterback Jim McMahon tossed to Payton. Payton headed to his left. His blockers opened a hole, and he bulldozed his way for six yards. He now had 12,317 yards in his career. This broke Jim Brown's record of 12,312.

Payton had always been hard to stop, even when he was in first grade in Columbia, Mississippi. One day his class was in line, ready to cross the street with the teacher. Walter didn't want to stay with everyone else. He took off running. The teacher shouted for the older boys to stop him.

"I just kept running faster, dodging and spinning away, stutter-stepping, keeping my balance, and running on," he remembered. "I made it, too, but the next day the teacher gave me a licking that wouldn't quit."[1]

Payton was a star running back in high school. Colleges all over the country offered him scholarships. He wanted to stay close to home and play for Jackson State in Mississippi.

His older brother Eddie was at Jackson. Eddie Payton later played in the NFL, too. When Walter was a senior, he and Eddie started a special workout of running up and down the levees along the Pearl River. They developed strong leg muscles and balance.

He broke almost every rushing and scoring record at Jackson State. He scored 113 touchdowns while he was there. The 66 touchdowns he scored in his senior year was an NCAA record. He was named Most Valuable Player in both the Senior Bowl and the East-West Shrine Game. Then he

Payton's nickname "Sweetness" did not fit his running style. He would bang into and bounce off defenders, making him one of the toughest backs to tackle.

was picked by the Chicago Bears in the first round of the 1975 NFL draft.

Payton's first year with the Bears was not spectacular. He only gained 679 yards on 196 carries. But the next year he gained 1,390 yards, and he barely lost the NFL rushing title to O. J. Simpson. In 1977 he did even better. He gained 1,852 yards and led the league. In a game against the Minnesota Vikings, he carried the ball 40 times for 275 yards. This was the most ever in a single game.

"He's the best back in football," Vikings coach Bud Grant said after the game. "I can't say anything about him that hasn't been said before."[2]

By the time he retired after the 1987 season, Payton had 16,726 yards. He also had set eight other NFL records. These included 110 rushing touchdowns and 77 games of 100 yards or more. His rushing and receiving touchdown total was 125. This was second only to Jim Brown's 126. Twelve years after retiring, Walter Payton died of a rare liver disease. He was forty-five years old.

Payton was not a graceful runner. He didn't bend his knees much. He swung his legs from the hip and ran almost on his tiptoes. His nickname was "Sweetness," but they didn't call him that because of his running style. He liked to bang into a defender and bounce or spin off. He seemed to really like crashing head-on into tacklers. He explained, "My coach at Jackson State, Bob Hill, always said, 'If you're going to die anyway, die hard, never die easy. Dish it out, hit the hitter.'"[3]

Although he was only five feet ten inches tall, Payton's upper body was heavily muscled. And he had enormous leg strength. Chicago backfield coach, Fred O'Connor, said, "God must have taken a chisel and said, 'I'm gonna make me a halfback.'"[4]

WALTER PAYTON

BORN: July 25, 1954, Columbia, Mississippi.

DIED: November 1, 1999, Barrington, Illinois.

HIGH SCHOOL: Columbia High School, Columbia, Mississippi.

COLLEGE: Jackson State College.

PRO: Chicago Bears, 1975–1987.

RECORDS: NFL All-Time Leading Rusher, 16,726 yards.

HONORS: Pro Football Hall of Fame, 1993.

Payton sneaks into the end zone for a touchdown against Dallas. In his thirteen years with the Chicago Bears, Payton set nine NFL records. He retired as the NFL's all-time leading rusher with 16,726 yards.

BARRY SANDERS

Sanders rushes for a first down. When he was a boy, many felt he was too small for football. But he has used his speed and power to run both around and over his tacklers.

BARRY SANDERS

IT WAS LATE IN THE game. Detroit Lions coach, Wayne Fontes, was nervous. The Green Bay Packers were within three points of the Lions, and they were driving once more. Then, Detroit recovered a fumble.

Fontes's assistant coaches began giving him advice right away. He cut the conversation short. "I don't care what you do," he shouted, "just give it to Barry."[1]

Barry Sanders was Detroit's rookie running back, and he was up to the challenge. He carried the ball six straight times. The last run was a one-yard touchdown that put the game out of the Packers' reach.

It must have been nice for Sanders to feel wanted. It wasn't always that way.

In his home town of Wichita, Kansas, he led his high-school team in touchdowns when he was a junior. But, people thought his older brother Byron was a better player. Barry set a school scoring record as a senior, but he was almost ignored by college scouts. He was only 5 feet 8 inches tall and weighed 180 pounds, so people thought he was too small. He received only two scholarship offers. He accepted the one to Oklahoma State University (OSU).

Sanders spent most of his first two seasons in college returning kicks and substituting for Thurman Thomas. Thomas was OSU's All-America runner. He finally got a chance to show what he could do when he was a junior. And he did plenty. He set major-college football's single-season rushing (2,553 yards) and touchdown (39) records. And he won the Heisman Trophy as the nation's best college player.

Sanders skipped his senior year in college to enter the

NFL draft. The Lions made him the third pick. He was just as good in the pros as he was in college. He gained one hundred yards or more in seven games in 1989. This was his rookie year, and he almost won the NFL rushing title.

He would have won the title, but he decided to sit out part of the final game because the Lions were far ahead. He has always put his team first. He doesn't have much interest in personal glory. Even when he won the Heisman Trophy, he did not want to take part in the televised announcement. He said he did not deserve so much attention. He gave his blockers all the credit for his success.

He did win the rushing title in 1990. More important, he led the Lions to the playoffs. Fontes changed Detroit's offense to get the ball to Sanders more often. "When you've got a Secretariat [the famous race horse]," he said, "you ride him."[2]

Sanders was not big—as pro running backs go—but he had tremendous leg strength. That gave him both speed and power. His running style was to try to keep away from tacklers as long as possible. When he couldn't, he tried to bowl them over. Some people compared his style to Walter Payton's. But Payton saw Sanders play and said, "I was never that good. He's better than I was."[3]

In 1997, Sanders won his fourth rushing title by gaining 2,053 yards, second best in NFL history. He also won the title in 1994 and 1996. On July 28, 1999, Sanders shocked the sports world by annoucing his retirement from the NFL at age thirty. At the time, he was only 1,458 yards shy of Walter Payton's all-time rushing record.

"Barry Sanders is one of those guys who shows you something you'll never see again," said Cincinnati Bengals linebacker James Francis. "He's one of those guys that comes along every ten years."[4]

BARRY SANDERS

BORN: July 16, 1968, Wichita, Kansas.

HIGH SCHOOL: North High School, Wichita, Kansas.

COLLEGE: Oklahoma State University.

PRO: Detroit Lions, 1989–1999.

HONORS: Heisman Trophy Winner, 1989; NFL Rookie of the
Year (NFC), 1989; NFL Co-MVP, 1997.

Although Sanders avoided the spotlight, he won several top honors including the Heisman Trophy and NFL Rookie of the Year. He captured the rushing title in 1990, 1994, 1996, 1997.

GALE SAYERS

ONE SATURDAY NIGHT IN DECEMBER 1965, Gale Sayers got a phone call from a friend. The friend told him that he had a chance to be selected NFL Rookie of the Year. But, he had to have a good game the next day against San Francisco.

Sayers had more than just a good day. He gained a record 336 combined yards in rushing, receiving, and kick returning. And his Chicago Bears thrashed the 49ers, 61–20. He also scored six touchdowns. This tied the NFL record set by Ernie Nevers in 1927.

After the game, San Francisco's Elbert Kimbrough said, "He doesn't have [Jim] Brown's power, but who needs power when you can run like that?"[1] And Ernie Nevers sent him a telegram that said: "Your brilliance will long be remembered in this sport."[2]

Sayers had always been a brilliant athlete. He grew up in Omaha, Nebraska. His family was so poor that he and his brothers cooked and ate sparrows that they shot with BB guns. Later, when he was in high school, he twice led the city in scoring. One reason, he said, was that each person who scored a touchdown received a certificate for a free hamburger at a local restaurant.

He had several scholarship offers, and he chose the University of Kansas. Sayers was an All-American running back when he was a junior and a senior. He set a single-game Big Eight rushing record when he gained 283 yards against Oklahoma State.

When Sayers finished college in 1965, the National Football League and the American Football League had not merged yet. Each year, the two leagues tried to outbid each other for

GALE SAYERS

Many feel that Sayers could have been the best rusher in the history of the NFL if a knee injury had not cut his career to only seven seasons.

the top players. Sayers was the top pick of both the Bears in the NFL and the Kansas City Chiefs in the AFL. He always wanted to play in the NFL, so he chose the Bears.

He had the kind of rookie season most players only dream of. He was second in rushing to the Cleveland Browns' Jim Brown. Sayers had 867 yards, and he set an NFL record with 22 touchdowns.

Sayers ran with a combination of speed, quickness, and agility. "He has wonderful speed," said Bears head coach George Halas, "and he has tremendous acceleration and a variety of gears. He can lull you into thinking he is going at top speed, and then turn it up another notch and be gone before you know it."[3]

In 1966, he led the league in rushing with 1,231 yards. This was a Bears record. And he caught 34 passes. The next year, he was third in rushing with 880 yards, even though he missed one game because of an injury.

Sayers might have set many more records, but in the ninth game of the 1968 season, he was injured. He took a hit on his right knee from the 49ers' Kermit Alexander. Three ligaments in the knee were torn. Sayers had to undergo surgery, and he was out the rest of the season.

After the surgery, he worked hard to get the knee back in shape. Amazingly, he once again led the league in rushing in 1969, with 1,032 yards. But now he mostly ran inside instead of sweeping around the ends. He could not cut sharply and escape defenders as easily as before. He retired after the 1971 season. It was only his seventh season in the NFL.

Sayers' name is not found among the NFL's all-time rushing leaders. But, some think that he was the greatest runner in history. "I thought I coached the two greatest backfields of all time," said former NFL coach Buddy Parker, "but Sayers is the best backfield all by himself."[4]

GALE SAYERS

BORN: May 30, 1943, Wichita, Kansas.

HIGH SCHOOL: Central High School, Omaha, Nebraska.

COLLEGE: University of Kansas.

PRO: Chicago Bears, 1965–1971.

HONORS: NFL Rookie of the Year, 1965.
Pro Football Hall of Fame, 1977.

Gale Sayers' quickness and agility made outsmarting and outrunning the defense easy. In 1966, he led the league in rushing with 1,231 yards.

O.J. SIMPSON

Simpson shakes off two tacklers. Even though he had a bone disorder in his legs as a child, he grew up to be one of the biggest and fastest rushers in football.

THE **NFL** SINGLE-SEASON RUSHING record! Two thousand yards in one year! Either one would be the highlight of a career. O. J. Simpson had them both, and he earned them in the same game.

December 16, 1973, was a cold, dreary day in New York. Simpson's Buffalo Bills were playing the New York Jets. O. J. needed 62 yards to break Jim Brown's record of 1,863. He needed 197 yards to reach the 2,000 mark.

The first 62 yards came quickly. In the first quarter, Simpson swept left end for 6 yards. Brown's record fell. Then, the Bills got the ball in the fourth quarter. Simpson gained 22 yards, then 9, then 4.

In the huddle, Bills quarterback, Joe Ferguson, told the team that O. J. needed just four more yards. He called "No. 5," a straight-ahead play. Fullback Jim Braxton would lead Simpson into the hole outside for seven yards. That made 2,003 for the season! It was a super running performance for a man who almost couldn't walk when he was a child.

O. J. stands for Orenthal James. It later became "Orange Juice" or just "Juice." He grew up in San Francisco's Potrero Hill district. He called it "your average black ghetto."[1] Because he had a bone disorder, he had to wear leg braces for years. Other kids called him "Pencil-Pins" because his legs were so skinny.

But those skinny legs were the fastest in the neighborhood. They had to be. O. J. Simpson was a tough kid who ran with a tough crowd. He often had to run from the police.

Simpson grew bigger and faster. He scored more touchdowns than anyone in the history of Galileo High

School. After high school, he went to a junior college. Then he transferred to the University of Southern California. In his senior year, he won the Heisman Trophy as college football's best player. "This not only was the greatest player I ever had," said Southern Cal coach John McKay, "but the greatest anyone ever had."[2]

Buffalo made Simpson the first player to be picked in the 1969 draft. He did not like Buffalo at first. The weather was cold and the Bills' coach, John Rauch, did not let him run the ball often. Lou Saban became the Bills' coach in 1972. He made Simpson the center of his offense. O. J. Simpson promptly gained 1,251 yards. He was the first American Football Conference back to go over 1,000 yards.

He led the NFL in rushing that year. He did it again in 1973 and in 1975. He retired in 1979 and became a television sports announcer. He had gained 11,236 yards in 11 seasons.

When Simpson began his pro career he was a reckless runner who liked to run over defenders. Later, he changed. "I don't believe in putting my head down and running over guys," he said. "If I have to for one yard, for a first down or a touchdown, I'll try, but I don't believe that when I step out on the field, I have to prove how much of a man I am."[3]

He was big enough to run inside with power, and he was fast enough to run outside. "You jam up your middle to stop him inside and he runs around you," an opposing coach once said. "You spread out to stop him from going outside, he goes right through you like a knife into butter."[4]

Like most great runners, Simpson ran by "feel." He wasn't taught. His junior college coach, Dutch Elston, said, "Nobody taught that boy how to run. Trying to teach him how to run would be like trying to teach Bing Crosby or Ray Charles how to sing . . . as a runner, he was a natural."[5]

O.J. Simpson

Born: July 9, 1947, San Francisco, California.

High School: Galileo High School, San Francisco, California.

College: University of Southern California.

Pro: Buffalo Bills, 1969–1977; San Francisco 49ers, 1978.

Honors: Heisman Trophy Winner, 1968; Pro Football Hall of Fame, 1985.

When he played with the Buffalo Bills, Simpson led the league in rushing three times and broke many NFL records.

EMMITT SMITH

DESPITE ALL THE EVIDENCE, THE jury was still out on rookie running back Emmitt Smith. The Dallas Cowboys made him their first round draft choice in 1990. Was he everything they hoped he would be? Would they have to wait two years for him to develop?

Then came the sixth game of the 1990 season against the Tampa Bay Buccaneers. Dallas had the ball on the Bucs' fourteen-yard line. Smith took the handoff and slid through a small hole. He followed two blockers, then he spun off one tackler and faked out another. Then he skittered into the end zone.

"I wasn't waiting any two years to see that," said Cowboys backfield coach Joe Brodsky.[1]

There should not have been any doubts. Smith was one of the most productive running backs in sports history. He gained 8,804 yards in four years at Escambia High School in Pensacola, Florida. He gained 4,232 in three years at the University of Florida. But, some pro scouts thought he was too slow.

"They never saw all those 90-yard runs of his in the peewee leagues," his mother said. "I never did see anyone catch him from behind once he had a ball under his arm."[2]

Emmitt had a ball under his arm almost from the time he was big enough to pick one up. He started playing tackle with his cousins when he was five. He began to play organized ball when he was seven. He rushed for 115 yards in his first game when he was a 5-foot-8-inch high school freshman.

Dallas coach Jimmy Johnson didn't think Smith was too slow. Johnson had tried to recruit Smith to go to the University

EMMITT SMITH

In just four seasons, Smith has helped turn the Cowboys into a championship team. Dallas won two consecutive Super Bowls, with Smith capturing the MVP award in Super Bowl XXVIII.

of Miami when he was coach there. It was now three years later. He had another chance. On draft day, Dallas made a trade to move up and take Smith at No. 17.

Smith was a starter by the second game of the 1990 season. Dallas began to let him run more often, and he rushed for 374 yards in the last four games. That was good, but the next three years were better than good. They were spectacular.

He gained 1,563 yards in 1991, the best record in the NFL. He did even better in 1992. He rushed for a league-high total of 1,713 yards.

In 1993, he missed the first two games of the season because of a contract dispute. Even with a late start, he led the NFL in rushing with 1,486 yards. He led the Cowboys to their second straight championship. He was named Most Valuable Player in the 30-13 Super Bowl victory over Buffalo.

Actually, the pro scouts were right. Smith does not have blazing, wide-receiver-type speed. He does have a great combination of power, agility, moves, balance, and speed. And all that still is better than average. His running style is one of going slow and waiting to see what develops.

In 1995, Smith led the league in rushing once again as the Cowboys won another Super Bowl. His 25 rushing touchdowns set an NFL record. "When Emmitt gets close to the goal line," said teammate Tommy Agee, "he's like a pit bull on a sirloin steak."[3]

Nobody enjoys watching Smith run more than his teammates, even when they're not supposed to. "One of the biggest mistakes I used to make was just watching him after I handed him the ball, instead of continuing the fake," said Dallas quarterback Troy Aikman. "He's amazing."[4]

Coach Joe Brodsky put it best. "He's magnificent," Brodsky said. "He'll take your breath away, and you won't get it back until he scores."[5]

EMMITT SMITH

BORN: May 15, 1969, Pensacola, Florida.

HIGH SCHOOL: Escambia High School, Pensacola, Florida.

COLLEGE: University of Florida.

PRO: Dallas Cowboys, 1990– .

HONORS: Most Valuable Player, Super Bowl XXVIII.

Smith sweeps around his blockers for a first down. Although he does not have the super speed of other running backs, his agility and moves have made him the key to the Dallas offense.

NOTES BY CHAPTER

Introduction
1. Murray Olderman, *The Running Backs* (Englewood Cliffs, N.J.: Prentice Hall, Inc., 1969), p. 4.
2. Mark Surfin, *Payton* (New York: Charles Scribner's Sons, 1988), p. 24.
3. Ibid., p. 36.

Jim Brown
1. James and Lynn Hahn, *Brown: The Sports Career of James Brown* (Mankato, Minn.: Crestwood House, 1981), p. 8.
2. Jimmy Brown, *Off My Chest* (Garden City, N.Y.: Doubleday & Company, Inc., 1964), p. 104.
3. Hahn, p. 26.
4. Ibid.
5. Gale Sayers, *I Am Third* (New York: Viking Press, 1970), p. 199.

Earl Campbell
1. John Devaney, *Winners of the Heisman Trophy* (New York: Walker and Company, 1990), p. 99.
2. Ibid., p. 102.
3. S. H. Burchard, *Sports Star Earl Campbell* (San Diego: Harcourt Brace Jovanovich, 1980), p. 51.
4. Sam Blair, *Earl Campbell: The Driving Force* (Waco, Tex.: World Books, 1979), p. 160.
5. David Kaplan and Daniel Griffin, *The Best of Bum: The Quotable Bum Phillips* (Austin, Tex.: Texas Monthly Press, 1980), p. 53.

Eric Dickerson
1. William Nack, "He Put the Squeeze on the Juice," *Sports Illustrated* (December 17, 1984), p. 18.
2. Nancy J. Nielsen, *Eric Dickerson* (Mankato, Minn.: Crestwood House, 1987), p. 8.
3. William Nack, "Mr. Smooth Rushes Into the Record Books," *Sports Illustrated* (September 4, 1985), p. 164.
4. "Eric Dickerson," *Lincoln Library of Sports Champions*, vol. 3 (Columbus, Ohio: Frontier Press Company, 1989), p. 27.
5. Ibid., p. 29.
6. Ibid., p. 24.

Tony Dorsett
1. Tony Dorsett and Harvey Frommer, *Running Tough* (New York: Doubleday, 1989), p. 121.
2. Dick Conrad, *Tony Dorsett: From Heisman to Super Bowl in One Year* (Chicago: Childrens Press, 1982), p. 35.
3. Ibid., p. 1.
4. Marcia McKenna Biddle, *Tony Dorsett* (New York: Julian Messner, 1980), p. 184.
5. "Tony Dorsett," *Lincoln Library of Sports Champions* (Columbus, Ohio: Frontier Press Company, 1989), vol. 3, p. 50.

Franco Harris
1. George Sullivan, *On the Run: Franco Harris* (Milwaukee, Wis.: Raintree Editions, 1976), p. 7.

2. S. H. Burchard, *Sports Star Franco Harris* (New York: Harcourt Brace Jovanovich, 1976), p. 49.

3. "Franco Harris," *Lincoln Library of Sports Champions*, vol. 16 (Columbus, Ohio: Frontier Press Company), p. 122.

4. Sullivan, p. 31.

5. *Burchard, p. 50.*

6. *Ron Reid, "Black and Gold Soul with Italian Legs," Sports Illustrated* (December 11, 1972), p. 37.

Walter Payton

1. Mark Surfin, *Payton* (New York: Charles Scribner's Sons, 1988), p. 39.

2. "Payton Runs All Over the Place," *Sports Illustrated* (November 27, 1977), p. 27.

3. Surfin, p. 7.

4. "Running Wild," *Newsweek* (December 5, 1977), p. 63.

Barry Sanders

1. Austin Murphy, "A Lamb Among Lions," *Sports Illustrated* (September 10, 1990), p. 64.

2. Peter King, "The Roar of the Lions," *Sports Illustrated* (October 14, 1991), p. 33.

3. "Lions' Running Back Barry Sanders Is `Better' Says Payton," *Jet* (January 8, 1990), p. 46.

4. "Lions' Barry Sanders Rushes for Team Mark," *Jet* (December 14, 1992), p. 47.

Gale Sayers

1. Paul Michael, *Pro Football's Greatest Games* (Englewood Cliffs, N.J.: Prentice-Hall, Inc., 1972), p. 189.

2. Gale Sayers, *I Am Third* (New York: Viking Press, 1970), p. 199.

3. Tex Maule, "An Extravagant Outing for a Rare Rookie," *Sports Illustrated* (December 6, 1965), p. 97.

4. "Gale Sayers," *Lincoln Library of Sports Champions*, vol. 14 (Columbus, Ohio: Frontier Press Company, 1989), p. 53.

O. J. Simpson

1. Bill Libby, *O. J.: The Story of Football's Fabulous O. J. Simpson* (New York: G. P. Putnam's Sons, 1974), p. 19.

2. Dorothy Childers Schmitz, *The Juice is Loose* (Mankato, Minn.: Crestwood House, 1977), p. 21.

3. Larry Fox, *Born to Run: The O. J. Simpson Story* (New York: Dodd, Mead & Company, 1974), p. 144.

4. Ibid., p. 62.

5. Bill Libby, p. 29.

Emmitt Smith

1. Gil LeBreton, "Offense Unleashes Emmitt," *Fort Worth Star-Tele*gram, *section 3 (October 8, 1991), p. 1.*

2. *Paul Zimmerman, "The 100-Yard Dasher," Sports Illustrated* (October 21, 1991), p. 76.

3. LeBreton, p. 6.

4. Tim Cowlishaw, "Dallas and Sense," *Smith & Street's Pro Football* (1993 edition), p. 10.

5. Zimmerman, p. 74.

INDEX